Dogs
That Help People

by Caleb Graham

HOUGHTON MIFFLIN HARCOURT
School Publishers

PHOTOGRAPHY CREDITS: Cover © Jim Craigmyle/Corbis 1 altrendo images/Getty Images. 2 © Photodisc/SuperStock. 3 ©John Nordell/The Image Works. 5 © Jim Craigmyle/Corbis. 6 © Paul Souders/Corbis. 7 Tracy Morgan © Dorling Kindersley. 8 Getty Images. 9 DAVID GRAY/Reuters /Landov. 10 ©PA/Topham/The Image Works. 11 altrendo images/ Getty Images. 13 Marmaduke St. John/Alamy. 14 © Jim Craigmyle/Corbis. (bkgd) © Photodisc/SuperStock.

Printed in China

ISBN-10: 0-547-25376-1
ISBN-13: 978-0-547-25376-3

9 10 11 0940 18 17 16 15 14 13
4500416911

Dogs are good friends to people. Dogs are fun to play with. Many dogs can even do tricks.

But some dogs are very special. These dogs help people.

Helper Dogs

People who have a disability cannot do some things other people can do. People with a disability sometimes need help, or assistance, to do some things.

Some dogs learn how to help people who have a disability. These dogs are called *assistance dogs*. Assistance dogs help people do things the people can't do by themselves.

assistance dog

An assistance dog helps a man who cannot see.

Guide Dogs

A guide dog is one type of assistance dog. Guide dogs are also called *seeing-eye dogs*. Guide dogs help people who cannot see. The dogs guide people when they are walking. The dogs help the people stay safe.

Laws for Guide Dogs

In many places in the United States, dogs are not allowed to go in restaurants or on buses and trains. But guide dogs can go in these places. There are special laws that let guide dogs go almost everywhere.

A guide dog is lying quietly in a restaurant.

Dogs like to be with other dogs and people.

Dogs have many traits that make them helpful to people. Dogs see and hear better than people do. Dogs have the ability to find things by smelling them. Dogs are also very friendly animals. They like to be with other dogs and people.

Some kinds of dogs make the best guide dogs. Guide dogs are usually big. That helps the dogs guide people through crowded places. Guide dogs also need to be strong. They must also do what they are told to do.

German shepherds and Labrador retrievers are good guide dogs. These dogs are strong. They are also very loyal. That means that the dogs will always stay friends with their owners.

How a Guide Dog is Trained

a Labrador retriever   a German shepherd

A Labrador retriever meets a German shepherd.

Most guide dogs start training, or learning, to help people when they are about one year old.

First, a person called a trainer teaches the dog the jobs it will need to do. The dog will learn to stop at street corners. It will learn to walk around things such as ladders and bushes. During training, a dog may whine. His legs may start to quiver, or shake. The dog has to practice over and over.

These puppies learn to follow their human partners.

Guide dogs learn to stay attentive even in busy places.

Guide dogs must learn not to do things they shouldn't do. A lot of things in the outside world can make dogs excited. Guide dogs have to stay calm even if there are loud noises or interesting smells around them. A guide dog cannot snap at people when it is upset or frightened.

A guide dog learns to guide a person past things that block the path.

Next, each dog meets a person who has a disability. This person becomes the dog's partner. The person and the dog start to learn together. A trainer is there to watch and help.

The dog and the person learn about each other. They learn to trust each other. They learn that they will take care of each other. The dog and the person together are a team.

Guide dogs must also learn to disobey, or do things they aren't told to do. That seems strange, but it's true!

A guide dog might need to disobey to save its partner's life. For example, a person who cannot see might be near a busy street. The person might tell her guide dog to walk across the street. But the guide dog might see that it's not safe to cross. So the guide dog must disobey.

A guide dog needs to keep its partner safe near busy streets.

When a guide dog finishes its training, the dog goes home to live with its partner. The partner helps the dog get to know its new home. The partner will make sure the dog meets other family members and friends. Soon the dog will feel comfortable and happy in its new home. The dog and its partner will feel connected to each other.

More Dogs That Help

Guide dogs aren't the only kind of assistance dogs. Some dogs help sick people. These dogs are called *therapy dogs*. Therapy dogs visit people in hospitals and other places.

Other dogs work with police officers. They patrol the streets together. The dogs need a rest at the end of a long work shift!

Two therapy dogs visit a boy at the hospital. Being friends with a dog can make people feel better!

A Free and Independent Life

People who have disabilities are just like everyone else. But they have to do some things differently. Guide dogs and other assistance dogs can help. These strong, smart dogs help people move around and live a free and independent life.

What an important job these dogs have!

Guide dogs help people go everywhere they want to go!

Responding

Author's Purpose

What was the author's purpose in writing this book? Copy the chart below. Write another detail from the book about things a guide dog does.

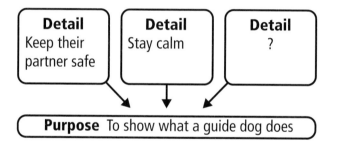

Detail
Keep their partner safe

Detail
Stay calm

Detail
?

Purpose To show what a guide dog does

Write About It

Text to World Think of jobs that school children can do to help other people. Write a paragraph describing one of those jobs.

ability	patrol
loyal	quiver
lying	shift
partners	snap

✔ **TARGET SKILL** **Author's Purpose** Use text details to tell why an author writes a book.

✔ **TARGET STRATEGY** **Summarize** Tell the important parts of the text in your own words.

GENRE **Informational text** gives factual information about a topic.